Mission used to be somethin
done by professionals in lands that ...
Such an idea was a fallacy then, but a laughable naivety today. We
face the undeniable reality of a post-Christian society, and our
population includes millions born in other nations. Mission has come
to us, and we as a UK church face not only growing numbers of people
who have never heard the gospel, but also growing hostility toward
our message, and our own waning confidence in it. Tim Chester
succinctly examines this most central question – what IS mission? He
comes up with some excellent parameters, and asks some provocative
questions with which we all should wrestle. If we are to be evangelicals
– that is, 'good news people' – then his treatment of this foundational
question is not just essential reading, but essential thinking also.
Jason Mandryk, speaker and author of 'Operation World'

This is another essential contribution from Tim Chester for anyone
thinking about reaching out to their community. Of course Christians
are going to be loving to the poor, the marginalized, the widowed.
But when we talk about mission, when we talk about the gospel, Tim
reminds us that we have to be intentional in pointing people to Jesus
the King and not only the values of the kingdom.
Graham Miller, CEO, London City Mission

With his usual readable clarity and style, Tim Chester both attacks
some misconceptions about the church's mission and affirms some
essential truths. He insists that since the lordship of Christ is over every
dimension of our lives, then the Great Commission (which is founded
on Christ's lordship) must impact every dimension of our life and work
as his disciples. So yes, everything has a missional dimension under

Christ's lordship. But he also and rightly insists that all our lives (and therefore whatever constitutes our mission in deed and word) must be integrated around the centrality of the gospel that affirms the uniqueness of Jesus of Nazareth as Lord and God and Saviour, and that announces the facts of what God has done through the whole Bible story to redeem humanity and creation. Everything then, in the life of a believer and of a church, should be missional, provided that everything is subject to the lordship of Christ and integrated around the gospel of the uniqueness of Christ. And what else does it mean to be a disciple?

Christopher Wright, International Ministries Director,
Langham Partnership International

Is Everything Mission?

Is
Everything
Mission?

Tim Chester

First published 2019

British Library Cataloguing-in-Publication Data
A catalogue record for this book is available from the British Library.

ISBN: 978-1-78974-108-7
eBook ISBN: 978-1-78974-109-4

Set in Avenir 11/15pt
Typeset in Great Britain by CRB Associates, Potterhanworth, Lincolnshire
Printed in Great Britain by Ashford Colour Press Ltd, Gosport, Hampshire

Introduction

In a world of unimaginable and unending need, what should be the priorities for our church outreach programmes? As mission organizations develop their strategies, what goals should they be aiming for?

For the forty-plus years that I have served in mission leadership, these debates have continued. The key issue is, what exactly is the mission of God in his world? Proclaiming the good news was taken as read. Surely that was the mission of God. Embracing social action as part of that mission, well, we were not so sure. Would it not inevitably, eventually, lead to the loss of our evangelistic heart? It didn't. A more holistic view of mission led to greater gospel fruitfulness.

For those same more-than-forty-years, a similar debate and struggle has gone on in my local church; a church known for preaching the good news, but not for significant social involvement. Should we have been more socially involved? Not everyone could proclaim the gospel but surely anyone could care for the poor or hold out a helping hand to the refugee. Again, as change to a more holistic practice took place, greater gospel fruitfulness was the result.

However, the danger is the pendulum swing. Community and social involvement might well get you a headline in the local paper. Proclaiming the good news probably won't. In leading a mission organization, I found Christians gave money more readily when presented with the picture of a starving child than when they were told of people starving spiritually because they were without God's word. The balance is hard to get and even more difficult to maintain.

The Keswick lectures have become an important feature of the annual Keswick Convention. It is an opportunity to have a more in-depth look at contemporary issues the church is grappling with. I am delighted that Tim Chester's excellent lecture, 'Is everything mission?' delivered at the 2018 Convention, is being published. The global mission of the church has always been, and continues to be, a primary emphasis of the Keswick Convention. Until every tribe and tongue has heard the great news of the Saviour, the call to go into all the world remains at the heart of the mission of God. In this lecture Tim does not attempt to cover every aspect of mission but he issues an important warning: 'A generation ago the challenge was to integrate social involvement into the task of the church. Today the challenge is to ensure that proclamation remains central.' Tim certainly argues for our dynamic engagement with the social issues and needs of our day, but is clear that if in that involvement we are not 'proclaiming Christ in some way shape or form – then it is not Christian mission'.

Today, as I look forward rather than back, I find myself living on a new housing estate. There are significant social and community needs. Litter picks, a food bank, mums and tots, and so much more will be a great blessing to this community. As God's people, we are called to bring a blessing and we have no greater blessing to give than the good news of Jesus. How can I ensure that in everything I do on this estate, Christ and his salvation are central?

Peter Maiden
Minister-at-large, Keswick Ministries,
and International Director Emeritus,
Operation Mobilisation.

Is Everything Mission?

Evangelicals in the nineteenth century had a great record of social involvement. William Wilberforce and John Newton campaigned against slavery. George Muller and Charles Spurgeon established orphanages in Bristol and London. William Carey, the pioneer missionary to India, did a bit of everything: he campaigned for women's rights and the humane treatment of lepers; he started savings banks to combat loan sharks, founded dozens of schools for boys *and* girls from all castes and pioneered lending libraries; he introduced new systems of gardening, reformed agriculture and published the classics of Indian literature; and that's just a sample of all that Carey did.[1]

However, for various reasons evangelicals lost their social conscience over the first two-thirds of the twentieth century. The welfare state created the impression that the care of the needy could be left to the government. The

---

1. Ruth and Vishal Mangalwadi, *Carey, Christ and Cultural Transformation: The Life and Influence of William Carey*, OM, 1993, 1–8.

'social gospel', a movement in the early twentieth century that redefined the church's task as building the kingdom of God entirely within history, meant social action became tainted by association. Perhaps most significantly, liberal theology put evangelicals on the back foot. They became a beleaguered minority within the wider church. As a result, it felt easier to hunker down in a ghetto rather then get out into the big, bad world with an agenda for reform. The historian Timothy Smith called this retreat 'the great reversal'. It seemed that evangelical Christians, once in the vanguard of social reform, had shifted into reverse and retreated from the world.

Things began to change in the second half of the twentieth century – evangelicals began to reverse the great reversal.[2] But still in the closing decades of the twentieth century, you had to make a case for Christian social involvement. Everyone accepted the need for evangelism; but social involvement was often viewed with suspicion. The great fear was that it would distract from evangelism. Of course, it was also hard to make a case *against* social involvement – everyone recognized the command to love our neighbour; but mission was seen exclusively as

2. See Tim Chester, *Awakening to a World of Need: The Recovery of Evangelical Social Concern*, IVP, 1993.

evangelism. Discipleship and training might also squeeze into definitions of mission as derivative activities; but many Christians doubted whether social involvement should be described as mission. The 'battle' was to get people to think beyond a narrow view of mission that saw mission as proclamation alone – a dualistic view that separated body and soul. Even when people acknowledged (or perhaps 'conceded') social involvement, many were reluctant to view it as mission. Mission was *not* everything.

That was the debate twenty-five years ago. Where are we now, twenty-five years on? The situation has, in some ways, *flipped*. What is in danger of being marginalized is no longer social involvement, but evangelism. A generation ago, the challenge was to integrate social involvement into the task of the church. Today, the challenge is to ensure proclamation remains central.

Let me identify two factors that may have contributed to this.

The danger of assuming too much

There is always a danger of a second generation no longer affirming what a first generation assumed. Twenty-five years ago, people would give talks and write books that said, 'Of course evangelism is vital, but we also need to be socially involved.' They did not stress the need for evangelism because they could take that for granted. What they stressed was the need for social involvement. It almost became a badge of an active and engaged Christian.

This is fine and understandable. The problem is the dominant note that the following generation hears is the emphasis on social involvement – so much so that the centrality of evangelism can be eclipsed.

Or think of it like this. We often stress our distinctives (the things that make us distinct). When evangelical Christians come together, there is much we hold in common: the person of Christ, the authority of Scripture, justification by faith alone. So, if I want to distinguish myself I talk about the few things – all relatively unimportant by comparison with those big commonalities – that are distinctive about me or my church or my organization. No-one says, 'Come and work with our organization because we believe in the deity of Christ.' You would look at them with a puzzled face and say, 'Everyone in the room believes that.' So instead we all focus on our distinctives: 'Come and work with us because we do church planting' or 'we work in Latin America' or 'we care for street children'.

Again, this is fine and understandable. The danger, though, is that our distinctives can become central, that secondary issues become primary identities. The declaration, 'What's different about us is our involvement in water projects or street children or environmental campaigning' can all too easily become 'water projects or street children or environmental campaigning are the key thing we do'. And in our zeal to raise support, that becomes 'this is the key thing *you* should do'.

The point is this: *we must not assume the gospel* and *must not assume gospel proclamation*. We need to make the gospel explicit and central to our identity, and we need to make gospel proclamation explicit and central in our ministries.

The threat of a hostile culture

We must be wary of assuming too much. However, perhaps the greater threat to evangelism is a wider social context that is increasingly hostile towards evangelism.

One aspect of this is **the threat of pluralism**. There are two kinds of pluralism. Pluralism as a *social phenomenon* is the fact that we now live with a diversity of cultures, ethnicities and worldviews. That is a great *opportunity* for the gospel. But the second kind of pluralism is the philosophical belief that all worldviews and religions are equally valid. That is a great *threat* to the gospel.

Chris Wright talks about 'the supermarket mentality'. We can walk into our local supermarket and choose between dozens of different breakfast cereals. He says:

> The supermarket mentality . . . dominates popular thinking about religion . . . [it] sees everything as a commodity and everybody as a consumer . . . Not surprisingly, then, this supermarket mentality is very critical of Christians who make claims about their faith and about Jesus which appear to deny the validity of other religions.[3]

As far as most people are concerned that is tantamount to saying, 'You can only buy my brand of cornflakes.'

Related to this philosophical pluralism is **the threat of relativism**. Relativism is the belief that there is no such thing as absolute truth, just different perspectives. The irony, of course, is that this is itself an absolute statement. And so, in the name of tolerance, our culture is increasingly intolerant to non-relativistic positions – like the gospel of Jesus Christ. In the past, tolerance was the conviction that, even when you disagreed with people, you should

---

3. Chris Wright, *Thinking Clearly About the Uniqueness of Christ*, Monarch, 1997, 12–13.

respect their right to hold their belief, and afford them political and social freedoms. Christians (especially non-conformist Christians) were in the forefront of developing this approach. Now, however, so-called tolerance has come to mean affirming the validity of every perspective, including every religious perspective. It is not acceptable to say that other people's moral or religious opinions are wrong. To say that other religions do not lead to God is seen as arrogant and any evangelism is deemed intolerant.

To this threat, we need to add **the threat of the new morality**. A generation ago, Christian ethics were main-stream. Of course, not everyone lived by them, but they defined the norms of our culture. Christian views of marriage, sexuality, the sanctity of life, gender roles and gender identity were all regarded as worthy ideals or at least valid options. But on all those issues, that situation has completely flipped round in the space of a gener-ation. Now the moral norms of our society include the *approval* of homosexual practice and gender reorienta-tion. To disagree with this is to be seen as *immoral*. In fact, within just the last twenty years our views have come to be seen, not just as marginal, but as deviant. Christians have become the immoral people in our culture. Charles

Chaput, the Catholic Archbishop of Philadelphia, says, 'People who hold a classic understanding of sexuality, marriage, and family have gone in just twenty years from pillars of mainstream conviction to the media equivalent of racists and bigots.'[4]

We have a new generation of young Christians who are battered by pluralism, relativism and the new morality. Think what that means for their attitude to evangelism. In some parts of the world, to stand for justice is liable to lead to imprisonment or violence. But generally speaking if you are a young Christian today in the West and you engage in social involvement, then your friends and colleagues will admire you. If you do a sponsored run to raise money for clean water or lobby for fair-trade products in your staff canteen or recycle your waste, then people will be impressed. They may or may not share your sacrificial attitude, they may not even always agree with the causes you espouse, but they will be impressed by your social concern. But if you evangelize, then you will be scorned and rejected. Your attempts at evangelism will put you in the same category as 'racists and bigots'.

This is why it is important to return to the question, *Is mission everything?* Do you want to be in the same

4. Charles Chaput, *Strangers in a Strange Land*, Henry Holt, 3.

category as 'racists and bigots'? Of course not. And so it is tempting just to do social action. And if we say mission is everything, then maybe social action is enough. If social action is mission then perhaps you can be content that you are being missional, that you are fulfilling the Great Commission, without ever involving yourself in the risky business of evangelism. Yet Jesus said:

> Woe to you when everyone speaks well of you,
>> for that is how their ancestors treated the false
>>> prophets.
>
> (Luke 6:26)

If you do what you do so people will speak well of you then it is probably not mission that you're doing.

So, *Is mission everything?* My answer is 'Yes' and 'No'. Everything *can* be mission, but it's not *automatically* mission. We will think about both the 'Yes' and the 'No'. I want to suggest that a focus on the person of Christ explains why everything *can* be mission, but why not everything is *automatically* mission. First of all, the 'Yes'.

1. The lordship of Christ = everything matters

'Jesus is Lord'. This statement was perhaps the first Christian creed. Paul says the message we proclaim is this:

> If you declare with your mouth, 'Jesus is Lord,' and believe in your heart that God raised him from the dead, you will be saved.
> (Romans 10:9)

'Jesus is Lord' is a declaration of *the divine identity of Jesus*. The word 'Lord' is the personal, covenant name of God – the name God revealed to Moses at the burning bush. So to declare 'Jesus is Lord' is to declare that the man Jesus is the Lord God.

'Jesus is Lord' is also a declaration of *the complete authority of Jesus*. Jesus has that authority *doubly*: as the divine King, but also as the human King. Through his death and resurrection, he has proved himself to be the Messiah. He is the Messiah God had promised to his people and the Messiah God has promised the nations. This is what Peter says on the Day of Pentecost:

> Therefore let all Israel be assured of this: God has made this Jesus, whom you crucified, both Lord and Messiah. (Acts 2:36)

This is what Paul says in the famous 'hymn' of Philippians 2:

> Therefore God exalted him to the highest place
>   and gave him the name that is above every name,
> that at the name of Jesus every knee should bow,
>   in heaven and on earth and under the earth,
> and every tongue acknowledge that Jesus Christ is Lord,
>   to the glory of God the Father.
> (Philippians 2:9–11)

This is what Jesus himself says in the Great Commission:

> All authority in heaven and on earth has been given to me. Therefore go and make disciples of all nations. (Matthew 28:18–19)

Already Jesus is acknowledged as Lord in heaven. Through his ascension, he entered heaven in triumph to receive all authority from his Father. But on earth his authority is still contested. The nations of the world still resist him. One day, God's will be done on earth as it is in heaven; but not yet. Mission, as defined in the Great Commission, is to call the nations to obedience. It is to proclaim Christ so that his authority, which is acknowledged in heaven, might also be acknowledged on earth. The place on earth where Christ is already acknowledged as Lord is the church. One day, every knee will bow. Whether people like it or not, Christ will be Lord on earth just as he currently is in heaven. Christians are those who gladly accept his lordship now.

The lordship of Christ means everything can be mission

Jesus is Lord of everything. He is not just Lord of our morality, our spirituality or our salvation. He is Lord of everything – our politics, our economics, our work, our parenting, our viewing and reading, our creating and art. So the call to repentance that we issue in mission embraces everything – every aspect of our individual and corporate lives; all our personal, political and economic relationships. If we are not calling people to this whole-life repentance then we are not preaching the whole Christ. Here is how John Stott summarizes what this involves:

> The two-word affirmation *Kyrios Iēsous* sounded pretty harmless at first hearing. But . . . it has far-reaching

ramifications. Not only does it express our conviction that he is God and Saviour, but it also indicates our radical commitment to him. The dimensions of this commitment are

- intellectual (bringing our minds under Christ's yoke),
- moral (accepting his standards and obeying his commands),
- vocational (spending our lives in his liberating service),
- social (seeking to penetrate society with his values),
- political (refusing to idolize any human institution)
- global (being jealous for the honour and glory of his name).[5]

It is not simply that mission involves calling people to submit their whole lives to Christ. This glad submission to Jesus then becomes part of the missionary dynamic. As our lives are lived under the lordship of Christ, so they point to that lordship. What this then means is that anything and everything can be done as a witness to Christ. Everything we do is to be done *under* Christ's authority and *for* Christ's glory.

---

5. John Stott, *The Contemporary Christian: An Urgent Plea for Double Listening* (Leicester: IVP, 1992). Quotation from John Stott, *The Essential John Stott* (Leicester: IVP, 1999), 419–420.

So mission is everything in the sense that it involves calling people to live every area of life in obedience to the lordship of Christ. And mission is everything because this obedience to the lordship of Christ then means every area of life is a potential testimony to the lordship of Christ. Every sphere of our lives is to *reflect* the lordship of Christ and thereby *testify* to the lordship of Christ. The Micah Declaration on Integral Mission puts it like this:

> Integral mission or holistic transformation is the proclamation and demonstration of the gospel. It is not simply that evangelism and social involvement are to be done alongside each other. Rather, in integral mission our proclamation has social consequences as we call people to love and repentance in all areas of life. And our social involvement has evangelistic consequences as we bear witness to the transforming grace of Jesus Christ. If we ignore the world we betray the word of God which sends us out to serve the world. If we ignore the word of God we have nothing to bring to the world.[6]

---

6. The Micah Declaration on Integral Mission was drawn up by 140 leaders from 50 countries in September 2001 at the inaugural consultation of the Micah Network, a global network of Christian relief and development agencies. See www.micahnetwork.org/integral-mission.

Let's look at an example of this in the Scriptures. In his first letter, Peter describes the church using some key Old Testament allusions:

> You are a chosen people, a royal priesthood, a holy nation, God's special possession, that you may declare the praises of him who called you out of darkness into his wonderful light.
> (1 Peter 2:9)

The church is now God's chosen people who, like Israel in the old covenant, have been chosen to be a blessing to the nations. The church is a kingdom of priests. Just as the priests made God known to the people so the church is a priestly kingdom whose lives and whose life together makes God known. The church is a holy nation, a company of people who reflect the holy character of God before a watching world. Finally, the church is a people who declare the praises of him who called them into his wonderful light. So mission is not the occasional activity of an enthusiastic few. It is the *identity* of all God's people. Every Christian is a missionary. So what then is our missionary strategy? Peter continues:

> Dear friends, I urge you, as foreigners and exiles, to abstain from sinful desires, which war against your soul.

Live such good lives among the pagans that, though they accuse you of doing wrong, they may see your good deeds and glorify God on the day he visits us.
(1 Peter 2:11–12)

We might summarize this as:

- Declare God's praises (2:10) – what we say.
- Abstain from sinful desires (2:11) – how we live.
- Do good (2:12) – what we do.

Mission involves what we say, how we live and what we do.

But verses 11–12 are just the headline. They summarize the strategy that Peter advocates. Then from verse 13 onwards, Peter outworks this big idea. He applies this mission strategy to:

- Our politics: 'Submit yourselves for the Lord's sake to every human authority: whether to the emperor, as the supreme authority, or to governors . . .' (2:13–17)
- Our work: 'Slaves, in reverent fear of God submit yourselves to your masters . . .' (2:18–25)
- Our homes: 'Wives, in the same way submit yourselves to your own husbands . . . Husbands, in the same way be considerate as you live with your wives . . .' (3:1–7)

Who does this mission and *where* do they do it? Ordinary Christians, in the context of ordinary life. In each area of life, bubbling under what Peter says is a concern that our conduct be shaped by the gospel so that, as Peter puts it in chapter 2:12, people might 'see [our] good deeds and glorify God'. To us all he says:

> Submit yourselves for the Lord's sake to every human authority . . . For it is God's will that by doing good you should silence the ignorant talk of foolish people.
> (1 Peter 2:13, 15)

Notice that word 'for'. Why do we submit to the authorities and honour political leaders? *So that* by doing good we might silence those who scorn the gospel. Peter speaks to slaves in a similar vein. The slave who 'bears up under the pain of unjust suffering because they are conscious of God' is someone suffering as a Christian (2:19). In the face of hostility, we bear witness to the Christ who suffered for us (2:21–25). And Peter's words to wives are particularly focused on those whose husbands 'do not believe the word' (3:1). Peter's aim is that 'they may be won over without words by the behaviour of their wives' (3:1). The word 'behaviour' here is the same word as that translated as 'lives' in chapter 2:12 (the sense of 2:12 is 'keep your behaviour good'). In other words, this is the application of chapter 2:12 to the specific context of the home. Let your conduct in your home point people to the glory of God. What does mission look like for the slave of chapter 2:18? It looks like submitting to his master and enduring unjust suffering. What does mission look like for the wife of chapter 3:1? It looks like submitting to her husband. It looks like 'a gentle and quiet spirit' (3:4). We reach a hostile world by living good lives in the context of ordinary life.

If your friend will accept an invitation to come to church with you on Sunday, then bring them along. However, my hunch is that nine out of ten times the person who lives in the house next door to you or sits at the desk next to you at work has refused your invitation to come. So take the gospel to them. Let your desk be the place where they see and hear the gospel. Let your home be the place where they see and hear the gospel. Indeed those who accept an invitation to come will almost certainly do so because they first saw your conduct in the workplace or the home.

Is mission everything? Yes, it can be.

2. The uniqueness of Christ = evangelism matters

However, we need to go further, and here we come to the 'No' part of our answer to the question of whether mission is everything. Some people say, 'Everything is mission' without qualification. 'I campaign against poverty. Campaigning is mission. Therefore I'm doing mission.' Maybe, but maybe not; after all, plenty of unbelievers campaign against poverty. Are they all engaged in the mission of Christ? Are they what we might call 'accidental missionaries'?

Some people want to define mission in incarnational terms. We are sent as God sent Christ. We need to be with people, like people, doing what they do. So, going to the pub and hanging out with your friends is mission. Is that correct? Maybe, but maybe not; it could just be hanging out with your friends. After all, if mission is just hanging out with friends then unbelievers are doing mission – probably better than you.

Christ must be at the centre of our mission. In the modern world, many people talk about mission. Companies have mission statements. Armies have a mission and warn against 'mission creep'. Governments send 'missions' to promote trade. What makes Christian mission distinctly Christian is *Christ*. What makes Christian famine relief or water projects or homeless shelters missional is Christ. Christ must be central because Christ is unique. The Christ-centeredness of our mission is the inevitable consequence of the *uniqueness of Christ*. If you believe in the uniqueness of Christ, then Christ will be central to your view of mission. Christian mission must have the proclamation of Christ at its centre.

Suppose a secular development agency drills a well and provides clean water in a village while a Christian agency drills a well and provides clean water in the neighbouring village. What is the difference? In some ways, there will be no difference. The engineering will be the same. The well may look the same. The water may be the same. But somewhere in the process the Christian agency will have (or should have) looked for opportunities to point to Christ.

Why is this important?

Christ provides a unique revelation

Only Christ is the image of the invisible God, God in human form, Immanuel, God with us, the Word made flesh. Christ is the one to whom God's revelation in Scripture points. He gives Scripture its meaning. There is no revelation of God apart from Christ. And so *if God is to be known, then Christ must be proclaimed.*

It is often said that the problem with defining mission is that the word does not appear in the Bible. We cannot look up chapter and verse to find a *biblical* definition of mission. But this is not quite true. For the word 'mission' comes from a Latin word that means 'sending'. A 'missionary' is 'a sent one'. And there is a Greek equivalent and it does appear in the New Testament. It is the word 'apostle' or 'apostolic'. The apostles are 'the sent ones'. So when the Nicene Creed says, 'We believe in one holy catholic and *apostolic Church*' the word 'apostolic' means both that the church is founded on the *authority* of the apostles and that it shares the *mission* or the 'sent-ness' of the apostles. The key point is that these two things go together: the apostolic *mission* goes hand in hand with the apostolic *revelation*.

God revealed himself uniquely in Christ. That is all well and good if you were there in first-century Judea to see and hear Jesus for yourself; but what about subsequent generations? How would God's revelation in Christ be accessible to everyone? Would we have to rely on hearsay? No, Christ chose the apostles to be his witnesses, to pass on God's revelation in Christ. And Christ empowered them with the Spirit for this task. They wrote their testimony to Christ through the inspiration of the Holy Spirit in the pages of the New Testament. The Holy Spirit worked in them and through them to ensure their record of God's revelation in Christ was reliable and authoritative. So the foundation of the church is the apostolic testimony in the New Testament and proclaiming the apostolic testimony in the New Testament is central to true apostolic mission.

So, to be missional or apostolic is to be sent by Christ to proclaim God's revelation in Christ as recorded by the first apostles in the pages of the New Testament (as well as God's revelation in Christ promised in the Old Testament). You do not have to hold a Bible in your hand all the time – not if you are digging a well – but you do have to have it to hand in your luggage. You do have to proclaim its message or open its pages at some point in the process if you are going to do *apostolic* mission – and there is no other authentic Christian mission. Consider the links in the chain of Paul's argument in Romans 10:

For 'everyone who calls on the name of the Lord will be saved'.

How, then, can they call on the one they have not believed in? And how can they believe in the one of whom they have not heard? And how can they hear without someone preaching to them? And how can anyone preach unless they are sent? As it is written: 'How beautiful are the feet of those who bring good news!'
(Romans 10:13–15)

Here are the inexorable links in Paul's argument:

1. Calling on the name of Jesus requires . . .
2. Believing in Jesus which requires . . .
3. Hearing about Jesus which requires . . .
4. Someone preaching Jesus which requires . . .
5. Someone being sent to proclaim Jesus.

Thankfully, someone has been sent by God to proclaim Jesus: you. This is why Paul quotes from Isaiah 52:7: 'How beautiful are the feet of those who bring good news!' Paul summarizes this 'chain' in verse 17: 'faith comes from hearing the message, and the message is heard through the word about Christ'. Faith requires hearing and hearing requires proclamation of 'the word about Christ'.

Christ provides a unique redemption

Christ was not just an educator who came to impart some information about God. Nor was he simply an inspiration or an example. First and foremost, Christ is the *Saviour* who dies for our sin, bearing God's judgment, reconciling us to God. As Jesus himself said of himself, 'The Son of Man came to seek and to save the lost' (Luke 19:10). Here we come to the old fault line between liberals and evangelicals. Is sin, as liberalism classically believes, a social malaise which human beings (inspired by the example of Christ) are to address? Or is sin, as evangelicals contend, an act of enmity against God, incurring his judgment, which can only be resolved by the sub-stitutionary death of Christ? Or, to put it another way, does Christ inspire us to save the world? Or is he the Saviour of the world?

I drove past a church recently that had as its slogan on the noticeboard outside the building, 'Agents of change'. That is kind of true. But if I am going to pick one line to sum up my church – its identity, its beliefs or even its activity – that is not where I want to start. The problem is that 'agents of change' makes *us* the good news. This is the key question: Is your gospel or your view of mission one which makes *you* the good news? Or is your gospel one which makes *Christ* the good news? Suppose this is your message: 'Inspired by Jesus, we are passionate about community transformation, social justice and environment care. Come and join us as we put the world right. Be part of the solution.' That is legalism. It may be cool, trendy, politically correct, right-on legalism. But it is still legalism. It says we can save ourselves or we can save our planet through our good works.

The true, biblical gospel tells us we are not the solution – we are the problem. The solution is Christ. Christ and Christ alone is the Saviour of the world. Yes, he inspires us. Yes, he is our example. But, first and foremost, he is our Lord and Saviour. I think there can often be a strange kind of inverted dualism in some social activism. In their personal lives, people look to Christ as their Saviour and on a Sunday they sing of how he saves. But in their professional life or their campaigning life or even their missional life they act as if it is our job to save the world. It is *not* our job to save the world. Our job is to *point* to the Saviour of the world.

The Lutheran theologian Carl Braaten says, 'Salvation is not whatever you want to call it . . . Salvation in the New Testament is what God has done to death in the resurrection of Jesus.' Chris Wright comments:

[Braaten] agrees that the Bible has plenty to say about the present experience and reality of salvation in this life. Nor does he exclude the physical, social and environmental dimensions of salvation ... But he rightly insists that unless the fundamental alienation of humanity from God, which the Bible calls death and attributes to sin, is dealt with, all other aspects of salvation remain ultimately cosmetic. And he rightly emphasises that the heart of the matter is resurrection – the historical resurrection of Jesus and the promised resurrection to eternal life of those who believe in him.[7]

This means that, unless we proclaim Jesus and life in his name, everything else we might do is ultimately what Wright calls 'cosmetic' because it does not address the fundamental issues of sin and death. Or, we might say, everything else we do is *temporary*. We can improve people's lives now, but only Christ gives *eternal* life. Only Christ saves from death and sin. This is precisely the point Peter himself makes at the end of 1 Peter 1:

Now that you have purified yourselves by obeying the truth so that you have sincere love for each other, love one another deeply, from the heart. For you have been

7. Chris Wright, *Thinking Clearly About the Uniqueness of Christ*, Monarch, 1997, 93–94.

born again, not of perishable seed, but of imperishable, through the living and enduring word of God. For,

'All people are like grass,

and all their glory is like the flowers of the field;

the grass withers and the flowers fall,

but the word of the Lord endures for ever.'

And this is the word that was preached to you.

(1 Peter 1:22–25)

Peter is quoting from Isaiah 40 – words spoken some 800 years before. So the work of Isaiah – which had been to proclaim the word of God – had already lasted 800 years. And, since we are now reading Isaiah words, we can add a further 2,000 years to that figure. But Peter's main point is that God's word lasts much longer than that. The impact of someone being born again lasts for eternity. Why? Because they are born again through the *enduring* word of God.

For all the good we can and *should* do in this world, we cannot create the world to come, nor prepare people for it other than to point to Christ. We can transform the metaphorical 'hell' in which people live now, but we cannot rescue them from the *eternal* hell of divine judgment. We can campaign for justice, but we cannot *justify* people before the judgment seat of Christ. We can ameliorate the effects of sin in people's lives, but we cannot wipe away the *guilt* of their sin. We can improve the next ten, twenty, thirty years of a person's life, but we cannot prepare them for the unending thousands of years that make up the life to come.

If I have to choose between improving someone's life now or proclaiming eternal life in Christ, then I will do the maths: 30 or 40 years verses eternity. Which matters more? As the 1982 Consultation on the Relationship between Evangelical and Social Responsibility (CRESR) put it in its final report:

> Evangelism relates to people's eternal destiny, and in bringing them good news of salvation, Christians are doing what nobody else can do . . . If we must choose, then we have to say that the supreme and ultimate need of all humankind is the saving grace of Jesus Christ, and that therefore a person's eternal, spiritual salvation is of greater importance than his or her temporal and material well-being.[8]

The context of proclamation

It is vitally important to add, though, that this is largely a hypothetical choice. The CRESR Report, quoted above,

---

8. *Evangelism and Social Responsibility: An Evangelical Commitment*, The Grand Rapids Report, Paternoster, 1982, 24–25.

prefaces the priority it gives to evangelism by saying, 'Seldom if ever should we have to choose between . . . healing bodies and saving souls.' It is the kind of the choice that you can pose in a classroom. But it bears little connection to the real world of mission. When you are in relationships with people, you do not have a hierarchy of needs all separated out so you can pick which one you address. Instead, you encounter people, and people do not have a soul and a body in two locations. What we encounter every time is embodied souls.

I have two daughters, and more than anything else I long for them to be converted. But that over-riding longing did not mean that as they were growing up, I neglected to feed and clothe them while I preached the gospel to them. I loved them and therefore cared for all their needs as best I could – though central to my interactions with them was a concern to present Christ through my life and words.

Peter says that new birth through the gospel is an imperishable act through an enduring word. However, it is striking that he employs this argument as a rationale for his call to 'love one another deeply, from the heart' (1 Peter 1:22). We are born anew into a new family and that brings new family responsibilities. In other words, as soon as you are *evangelistically* involved in a person's life, then you are going to be drawn into caring for *all* their needs.

This is why the language of 'priority' is not always helpful. Some people want to say that both evangelism and social action are part of mission, but evangelism has priority. This, however, implies discrete activities, some of which are unimportant or optional. We prioritize tasks by ordering them in a list. The implication is that the tasks at the bottom of the list can be safely left undone if we lack time or resources. But gospel proclamation always takes place in a context. There is the context of eternity which gives it such weight. But there is also the wider context of the lives of the people to whom we are speaking which we cannot ignore. There is also the context of our own lives as speakers, which must match the message we proclaim. We must care for the whole of a person's life and the whole of our lives must testify to Christ.

Think about how Paul describes his ministry among the Thessalonians: 'Because we loved you so much, we were delighted to share with you not only the gospel of God but our lives as well' (1 Thessalonians 2:8). The reality of mission on the ground involves sharing our lives *and* sharing the word.

The centrality of proclamation

Therefore, a better term to capture the vital importance of sharing the word of Christ is 'centrality'. The uniqueness of Christ's revelation and the uniqueness of Christ's redemption mean words must be central to Christian mission. We must proclaim Christ.

People often quote John's 'great commission' as a justification of a broad understanding of mission. In John 20:21, Jesus says, 'As the Father has sent me, I am sending you.' This, people argue, means mission is doing anything Jesus did. However, this ignores both the immediate and broader context. In the immediate context the focus is on proclaiming the forgiveness of sins (John 20:23). In the broader context, John structures his Gospel around a number of signs – miracles that Jesus performed that point to his identity. But each of those signs must be interpreted. John, for example, tells the story of the feeding of the 5,000 and then records how Jesus went on to explain that he himself is the bread of life.

The same is true of the good works we do – they need interpretation if they are to point to Jesus. Otherwise we will be like signposts pointing nowhere. Or, worse still, we point in the wrong direction; we will point to ourselves and our good works. People will assume we care for the poor or campaign for justice because we believe this life is all that really matters or because we believe we are saved by our good works.

So proclamation must be central. Words without deeds are poor mission; deeds without words are not mission at all. What makes Christian mission Christian is the proclamation of Christ. This is not a justification for bad, uncontextual or manipulative evangelism. It does not mean we need to proclaim the gospel all the time. But if we are not proclaiming Christ – in some way, shape or form – then it is not Christian mission.

At this point, someone might say, 'What about the diversity of gifts within the church? Surely God has gifted some people for social action and others for evangelism?' Let me make two responses. First, I agree that some people are especially gifted as evangelists. But every Christian can and should speak of Christ. I do not expect everyone to give a sermon or provide an apologetic. But I am asking you to speak of the beautiful Lord and Saviour who loved you, died for you, rescued you and keeps you. Second, since some people are gifted evangelists, let's make mission a *communal* endeavour. If you are running a social action project then ensure there is an evangelist on your team. Invite people into the community life of your church so they meet the natural evangelists among you. You may find it hard to challenge people to put their faith in Christ, but you can invite them to come to church or introduce them to other Christians. What we must avoid is social action in one location and evangelism in other location, as if they are separate and unrelated activities.

It might be helpful to recognize that integrating evangelism and social action often involves two options, which are both valid. Suppose you heed the call to pursue justice by getting involved in campaigning against modern-day slavery. You have a choice. You could get involved in a Christian group that speaks in Christ's name and proclaims the gospel to those in need it seeks to help. Alternatively, you could get involved in a non-Christian group and evangelize your co-belligerents. As you talk about what drives you – glad obedience to the lordship of Christ – you will be able to speak of your Saviour. Both these options are good options; both create opportunities for gospel proclamation.

Turn back to 1 Peter and something that might look like an exception to the centrality of evangelism. As we have seen, Peter says to wives:

Submit yourselves to your own husbands so that, if any of them do not believe the word, they may be won over

without words by the behaviour of their wives, when they
see the purity and reverence of your lives.
(1 Peter 3:1–2)

At first sight, that looks like you do not need words. Peter
specifically calls these women to a life 'without words'.
But we can assume that the wife here has already spoken
of Christ so that words are *already present* in this context.
The scenario is a wife whose proclamation of Christ has
been rebuffed. What does she do next? She gets on with
being a good wife. She backs up her words with her
behaviour. She gives her husband a hundred reasons to
re-open the conversation that previously he has shut down.

This leads us to the climax of this section on mission in
1 Peter, the famous words of chapter 3:15:

> But in your hearts revere Christ as Lord. Always be
> prepared to give an answer to everyone who asks you to
> give the reason for the hope that you have. But do this
> with gentleness and respect, keeping a clear conscience.
> (1 Peter 3:15)

Notice, again, that we begin with the lordship of Christ.
We are to revere Christ as Lord in *every* area of our lives.
And Peter's expectation is that this will then generate
questions from the watching world and we will need to

be ready to give an answer. Is everything mission? It is if your conduct is raising questions and you are giving Christ as the answer to those questions.

This is so important in our current cultural context. Peter continues in chapter 3:16: 'so that those who speak maliciously against your good behaviour in Christ may be ashamed of their slander.' These words echo Peter's headline principle back in chapter 2:12: 'Live such good lives among the pagans that, *though they accuse you of doing wrong*, they may see your good deeds and glorify God on the day he visits us.' We live in a culture, as we have noted, in which we are routinely accused of doing wrong. For many of us, what Peter says in chapter 4:3–4 describes our everyday experience:

> For you have spent enough time in the past doing what pagans choose to do – living in debauchery, lust, drunkenness, orgies, carousing and detestable idolatry. They are surprised that you do not join them in their reckless, wild living, and they heap abuse on you.
> (1 Peter 4:3–4)

That is exactly what's happening today: people are abusing us for not affirming their reckless immorality. What is our response to be? To do good and to speak of Christ. God has chosen you and called you 'that you may declare the praises of him who called you out of darkness into his wonderful light' (1 Peter 2:9).

Is mission everything? Yes, as long as the proclamation of the saving name of Christ is at the centre.

Reflection Questions

1. How can we encourage one another to keep speaking of Christ in the face of increasing hostility toward evangelism?

2. John Stott calls on us to bring the intellectual, moral, vocational, social, political and global dimensions of our lives under the lordship of Christ. In each case, identify one way in which Christ's lordship is changing your life.

3. 'Every sphere of our lives is to *reflect* the lordship of Christ and thereby *testify* to the lordship of Christ.' How is your life testifying to the lordship of Christ at the school gate, at work, in the gym, in your book group or retirement community, in your leisure time?

4. 'We need to make gospel proclamation explicit and central in our ministries'. What does that look like for your mums and tots group, your seniors' ministry, and the youth group? What does it mean for the ministry you are involved in?

5. How can we ensure an emphasis on the mission field on our doorsteps does not lead to a neglect of the needs of unreached people groups?

6. Suppose a Christian friend asks you to help them decide whether to give a week of their holidays to help with (1) a Christian camp, (2) a beach mission, (3) a local environmental project, (4) a church-run project to tidy the gardens of elderly neighbours or (5) a government-run holiday club for disadvantaged children. How would you advise them?

7. What should make Christian social action distinctive from the activities of other groups?

8. Can you think of examples of social action creating evangelistic opportunities?

9. How can we ensure our social action points to Christ and not to ourselves, that we make him – not us – the good news?

10. Suppose you're on the global mission committee of your church and you've received requests from (1) a church planting team in France, (2) a street children's project, (3) a missionary to an unreached people group, (4) a Bible translator and (5) an environmental project. How are you going to decide how to allocate the money?

For more on these issues, see:

- Tim Chester, *Good News to the Poor: Sharing the Gospel Through Social Involvement* (IVP).
- Tim Chester, *Mission Matters: Love Says Go* in the Keswick Foundations Series (IVP).